When God and I Speak:

Intimate

Conversations

TANYA AMEY

A 31-Day Devotional

When God and I Speak: Intimate Conversations
A 31-Day Devotional
©Copyright 2017 Tanya Amey

Hot coffee cup with hearts icon made by Freepik from
www.flaticon.com

ISBN 978-0-692-98337-9 (paperback edition)

Dedication

This devotional is dedicated to all those who have had difficulty with prayer. Having heard several testimonies of how these devotions have provided encouragement and a springboard to initiate one's own prayer life, it is my prayer that those reading this will be inspired to go deeper in their relationship and conversations with God. God desires to speak with us and doesn't expect eloquent, perfect speech; He wants to know about our day, what our likes and dislikes are, and He desires to answer and share with us through His Word. Be encouraged, dear reader that as you draw near to God, He will draw near to you. Happy conversing!!

Thank You

Heavenly Father, thank You for encouraging conversations with Your creation. Thank You for desiring to speak to us and Your willingness to hear us when we speak. Thank You for giving me a platform to use my voice and my time with You as a point of contact for others to cultivate, develop and deepen their conversations with You. I am still in awe that this is really happening and I pray that I can continue to make You proud.

To my husband, Michael, thank you for believing in me, pushing me, cheering for me, loving me, correcting me, helping me, and supporting me in all that I do. This is a win for both of us and I am looking forward to the opportunity to support you in the same way when you write your books. I love you.

To my children, Michael II, Jazmyne and Chloé, thank you for being patient with mommy and allowing me to teach you how to speak to God through prayer. Thank you for contributing to my devotions and for teaching me how to be a better mom each day. Thank you for loving me and allowing me to love you. I hope to make you proud as much as I am proud of you.

To my parents, Dad and Mom, you have always been in my corner and this project is no exception. Thank you for your unending faith and love in whatever I do. Thank you for not only supporting and encouraging me with your words, but for supporting and encouraging me with your finances. Your financial investments mean so much to me and have helped bring this idea to life.

To Dad and Mom Amey, thank you for cheering me on and for your continuous prayers. As I always say, "I've been blessed with the best!"

To Apostle and Dr. Betty Price, thank you for your consistent commitment to the body of Christ. You have set the standard and have taught and continue to teach me valuable life lessons. Thank you for the innumerable deposits you have made and continue to make in me spiritually and naturally; for the wisdom, guidance, understanding and love. I will continue to pursue a life that is pleasing to God. To my Apostle and Dr. Betty, I honor you. THANK YOU!

To my covering and mentors, Drs. Michael and DeeDee Freeman. Thank you for covering us, loving us and supporting us. There are truly no words to describe what your roles in our lives mean to me. I am excitedly looking forward to the future and the opportunity to continue to learn, grow and develop under you. Thank you Dr. DeeDee for your mentorship, I don't take it lightly or for granted. Thank you for writing the forward; it means so much to me. I appreciate you.

To Juliette, Katrina, Norbert, Erica and Audrey, thank you for lending your skills and expertise in helping me get this project done! Only God could have orchestrated and placed you in my life for such a time as this. I sit in awe at how you each embody the true spirit of giving – having given of your time, skill, ideas, encouragement and love. I am truly thankful.

To Mama Lori and Tracy, thank you for believing in me and using your time and expertise to make sure I am a success. I appreciate you.

To my Koi Family, thank you for pushing me and encouraging me to give all that I can. You challenge me to go beyond my natural limitations and reach for unthinkable dreams. You make me smile and I am happy to be doing life with you.

To all my family, friends and readers, thank you for believing in me! This one is for YOU!

Contents

Foreword

Unfortunately, in this age of social media craze, many (including believers) have turned to their social media pulpit to express and gain insight totally ignoring God's command to seek Him first (Matthew 6:33). Blinded by the fact that 80% of their followers have no righteous resolve for any situation they face. But through her passionate project of *Intimate Conversations*, Tanya allows her readers to become a part of her transparent relationship with the Father.

I commend her on publishing this needed tool. Prayer has and always will be the foundation to your ever growing relationship with our Father. I have personally built my own life on this principle and I am currently witnessing the fruit of it in the life of Tanya and her family.

My desire is that you don't treat this book as just another prayer book but rather put it in your daily tool kit and watch your intimate time with the Father flourish!

Dr. DeeDee Freeman,
Spirit of Faith Christian Centre, Maryland, USA

Introduction

I remember sitting in our hotel room after attending a women's conference and being so confronted and challenged by the information that was shared; I felt like there was something that I had to do. I remember going to bed that night and having a vivid dream about being in a fight and having all the weapons that I needed but not knowing how to operate them. When I woke from the dream, God began to share with me how many believers are equipped with the necessary tools, yet find themselves defeated because they don't know how to use them. One of the weapons is prayer!! Prayer is one of a believer's greatest tools in living this life victoriously.

It was in that moment that I began to document how I pray. Prayer has been and always will be a part of my life, but this assignment was different. I was compelled to take my everyday issues, challenges, shortcomings, successes and victories and share them with the world. I began to share my conversations with God through prayer virtually. What I thought may be an every now and again post, became more than 365 days of public, intimate conversations. It was from these vulnerable posts that I was encouraged to write this devotional. The testimonies on how my transparency unlocked a passion for prayer and spoke to the very core of the readers and situations they faced were enough to inspire this piece. This is not meant to only be a devotional but a tool in which I aspire to help those who may be struggling with prayer, find their voice. This is also where I share my journey on how I prayed through some of my most challenging times. Prayer is a conversation between you and God. As you speak, He listens and when He speaks, He speaks through His Word. As you read through these pages, take an assessment on where you are in your life right now, and begin your conversations with God, Who desires to hear from you. Remember that you are equipped with the greatest tool anyone can have and that is the power through prayer.

DAY ONE

Relax

I think that we, as a people, have become too consumed in the sensationalisms of this society. Things like media, our jobs, responsibilities and the like have caused us to brush through life in order to produce results. I wonder if the process of our successes and accomplishments can be recalled at will; or have we become so conditioned with "getting things done", that we don't take the time to enjoy the steps it took to get there? What if, instead of trying to keep up with everyone else, we focused on keeping up with ourselves and what it is we want to accomplish from day to day? When we give attention to our desires and passions, we realize that in doing so, we can help many people. However, when we spend our time focusing on what other people are or aren't doing, we tend to lose track of ourselves and what we are purposed to do.

Time is going to pass, whatever we do; so can I encourage us to relax, slow down long enough to enjoy the moments that await us and find a sense of accomplishment in that. I trust that as you take a breath, take a moment for yourself and just relax; you will realize that you can actually find pleasure in what life has to offer.

Prayer

Our most gracious and kind Father, we do thank You for the bountiful opportunities that we have in learning to appreciate this life that You have blessed us with (John 10:10). Help us to take a moment to slow down, breathe and consider the wonders of Your spectacular creations. We focus on You and not on the things that would take our attention off of You (Colossians 3:2). We know that time will pass, but may it pass with us having appreciated the moments. We rest in knowing that You have given us all things richly to enjoy (1 Timothy 6:17) and therefore we will not waste another moment with the things that will have no eternal impact. In Jesus' Name, Amen.

Set your affection on things above, not on things on the earth.
Colossians 3:2

What things have taken your attention off your purpose? Identify those purpose distractions and counteract them with purpose enhancers. Ask God to help you fulfill purpose more than you do the things that will delay you in fulfilling your purpose.

_____

_____

_____

_____

_____

_____

_____

_____

_____

_____

_____

_____

_____

_____

_____

_____

DAY TWO

Tired

Having young children, your days and nights can be completely unpredictable. There's a required attention needed all the time and your only response is to respond.

The other night, seemingly out of nowhere, our daughter, Jazmyne, complained of tummy pains. Initially we brushed it off because it seemed most convenient that there were tummy complaints when it was time for bed. It wasn't until after we were into an amazingly deep sleep that we heard the sound of this tummy ache manifesting as we woke to find our little girl in the bathroom vomiting. There was only time to respond by ensuring she felt comforted with our presence and prayers. After we cleaned her up and got back to sleep, we found ourselves repeating this process because this happened over and over again, throughout the entire night. Needless to say, having to wake up and prepare our eldest for school the next morning was quite a struggle. We were all tired! I'm not even sure if tired is a fair description. We were deprived of sleep that was desperately needed for functioning. What's interesting is that no matter how exhausted we were, we still responded to her needs and the needs of our son. We also made a point to maintain our morning devotions and prayers.

There are times where we are tired and burnt out, but we will still need to respond to the responsibilities and expectations that await us. However, I realized that my rejuvenation and refreshing came as a result of ensuring that I spent time with my Heavenly Father. I'm not saying that I'm not tired; I'm saying that in the midst of tiredness, I found the strength and refreshing I needed to get me through the tasks that needed my attention. So may I encourage you to not let tiredness or fatigue keep you from getting the ultimate refreshment from the

Source of our strength. Fill yourself up by spending time with God and you will find that you have the energy and stamina to face whatever comes your way.

Prayer

Heavenly Father, You are the Source and Strength of our lives (Psalms 27:1). You do for us more than we could ever do for ourselves. You rejuvenate us and strengthen us to go beyond our human limitations. We thank You that in Your presence there is fullness of joy and at Your right-hand pleasures forevermore (Psalms 16:11). Thank You for refreshing and giving rest to the weary (Isaiah 28:12). We don't try to do things in our own ability and in our own strength; we completely rely on and trust in You. In Jesus' Name, Amen.

> **To whom He said, "This is the rest with which You may cause the weary to rest," and, "This is the refreshing," Yet they would not hear. Isaiah 28:12**

God desires to give you rest. The question is, will you come to Him and allow Him to refresh you? What areas can you identify right now that have you tired? Jot them down and ask God to give you rest and refreshing in those areas.

_____

_____

_____

_____

_____

_____

_____

_____

_____

_____

DAY THREE

Cravings

Have you ever experienced a desire for something, a craving? It's said that during pregnancy one can have extreme cravings and after having three pregnancies, I can recall my desire for certain foods and drinks being very strong and persuasive. I've spoken to other moms who've also shared their strange craving stories. There were times my husband would also have cravings during my pregnancies. Apparently these cravings are a result of what the growing baby needs or desires while developing, which is why moms will say they're "eating for two."

In hindsight, I think that though hormones have a part to play, pregnancy is the only real excuse to eat what you want, whenever you want and as often as you want, without criticism. Not every pregnant person experiences cravings, but for some, the cravings are very real. Can I encourage us to stay pregnant with God's heart for us and keep hungering, thirsting, desiring and craving for Him and Him alone. I believe in doing so, He will ensure that we remain forever satisfied.

Prayer

Heavenly Father, You satisfy our mouths will all good things (Psalms 103:5) and we thank You. Thank You for showing us how to use our words and our voices. As a deer pants for water, God, so our souls long and thirst for You (Psalms 42:1). We do not starve nor dehydrate ourselves from what we know we need and that is Your Word. For we are sure to receive our daily bread which You give (Matthew 6:11). Fill us up to overflowing as we drink from Your well that never runs dry. For we know that Jesus is the Bread of Life and we who come to

Him will never hunger and we who believe in Him will never thirst (John 6:35). In Jesus' Name, Amen.

> ***And Jesus said to them, "I am the bread of life. He who comes to Me shall never hunger, and he who believes in Me shall never thirst." John 6:35***

What are some of the ways you can hunger and thirst more for God?

_____

_____

_____

_____

_____

_____

_____

_____

_____

_____

_____

_____

_____

_____

_____

_____

_____

_____

_____

_____

_____

_____

DAY FOUR

Favor

Favor isn't fair, nor does it have to be. I want God's very best for my life, my family's lives and everyone I'm associated with, without apology. Too often, people are made to feel ashamed or guilty when they receive blessings, but we mustn't forget that blessings are a part of our covenant promise. I want the fulfillment of Scripture made manifest; that surely goodness and mercy will follow me all the days of my life, that I will live my days in prosperity and my years in pleasure.

There is no reason for us to dumb down receiving God's goodness and new mercies every morning. As a matter of fact, it's something we should be looking forward to. We need to reverse our thinking when it comes to receiving the blessings that are promised to us and view it as an opportunity for others to see that we serve a good God who wants to bestow abundance over His people. My prayer is that we stay in a mode of expectancy, looking for our blessings as we look for ways to be a blessing to others.

Prayer

Heavenly Father, we know that everything You make is good (Deuteronomy 26:11). Thank You for making good what the enemy means for evil (Genesis 50:20). We do not apologize for the goodness and mercy that is provided for us anew every morning. We believe and anticipate Your Word, that surely goodness and mercy will follow us all the days of our lives (Psalms 23:6). We expect nothing less than Your richest blessings in our lives. We forgo walking around with false humility in not having enough for we know that Your blessings makes one rich and adds no sorrow (Proverbs 10:22). We also boast in You and Your goodness towards us to set an example to others on how well You care for Your people. We are unapologetically and enthusiastically looking forward to Your showers of blessing over us and that we have opportunity to represent You as we bless others. In Jesus' Name, Amen.

> *The blessing of the Lord makes one rich, And He adds no sorrow with it. Proverbs 10:22*

What have you been blessed with today? Write it down and thank God unapologetically.

_____

_____

_____

_____

_____

_____

_____

_____

_____

_____

_____

_____

_____

_____

_____

_____

_____

_____

_____

DAY FIVE

Make Room

There are so many things that I am believing God for. There is such an expectancy and excitement that looms in the atmospheres surrounding people who are believing God for specific things. With the expectancy and excitement, we will receive nothing, if there is no space for it. It's possible to delay our receiving because we have no place for what it is that we are believing for. We need to declutter, organize and make space, because if we are expecting blessings that will overwhelm us, according to Amos 9:13 in The Message translation, we don't have time to purge as we go. We need to prepare a place now and when we do, I believe we will see the flood of blessings come our way.

Prayer

Heavenly Father, our God, Who is able to do exceedingly, abundantly above all that we could ever ask or think (Ephesians 3:20); we thank You in advance for Your innumerable blessings. We know and believe that whatever things we ask for when we pray, we believe we will receive them at the point of prayer, and have complete faith that we have those things now (Mark 11:24). We are exceedingly glad and expectant for what is to come. We are so expectant, that we make a place for what it is we have prayed for. We thank You that there will not be enough room to receive that in which is coming our way (Malachi 3:10). We make space for the overwhelming overflow by organizing our lives and decluttering areas that will be required for the abundance. We thank You in advance and are looking forward to the blessings that will overtake us (Amos 9:13 MSG). In Jesus' Name, Amen.

**Therefore I say to you, whatever things you ask when you
pray, believe that you receive them, and you will have them.
Mark 11:24**

Write down what you are believing God for and begin to make the space for
its manifestation.

_____

_____

_____

_____

_____

_____

_____

_____

_____

_____

_____

_____

_____

_____

_____

_____

_____

_____

_____

_____

_____

New Beginnings

Have you ever had to start something new or begin again and weren't sure of all it would require or even if you'd be able to accomplish it? Despite how you felt, you decided to endure and go with it, and to your surprise you were actually quite good at it? This should encourage us to not be afraid to take risks, try new things, start again and develop a new normal. Life is all about exploring and trying new things. I heard it said this way, "you grow when you try something for the first time." So don't be afraid to try something new, because even if all else fails, you can rest assured that you've grown.

Growth in any area is a sign of maturity and maturity indicates that you have moved from one level to another. Fear of pursuing and taking risks will cripple, stunt and even kill growth. We can't allow the things that we are unsure of to hinder us from taking a step that has the potential to unlock eternal destinies and unlimited abundance.

Prayer

Most Holy God, You are the Alpha and Omega, Beginning and the End, the First and the Last (Revelation 22:13) and it is You we worship and adore. You have created us on purpose with a purpose and it is our mandate to pursue it. Before we were born, You knew and formed us in our mother's womb (Psalms 139:13, Jeremiah 1:5), therefore You know more about us than we know about ourselves. Transfer Your knowledge to us. We are not timid, scared or hesitant to move forward in the dispensation of grace that You have bestowed upon us to complete our tasks (Ephesians 3:2). May we take on each new challenge with

Your all-sufficient grace and trust that You Who has begun a good work in us is well able to complete it (Philippians 1:6). In Jesus' Name, Amen.

> *Being confident of this very thing, that He who has begun a good work in you will complete it until the day of Jesus Christ. Philippians 1:6*

Being that the work in us begins and ends with Christ Jesus, what are some things that you can do for the first time?

_____

_____

_____

_____

_____

_____

_____

_____

_____

_____

_____

_____

_____

_____

_____

_____

_____

_____

_____

_____

_____

DAY SEVEN

Snapback

Social media has coined a term "SnapBack" or "dap back" as a way to quickly and sharply respond to a negative comment made to or about you. What if we took these negatively connotative terms and looked at them as a way to showcase maturity? Instead of responding negatively, quickly or sharply, what if we responded with prayer or a soft answer? Not lessening ourselves to the behavior of our haters or critics allows our positive living to speak volumes. For many, this requires self-control. This exercise of self-control is powerful because it puts you in a position of authority and victory. When we give people license to cause us to respond negatively, it speaks more to our lack of control than to their childish behavior. There's power in silence and greater victory in prayer. If more of us would be quiet, pray and focus on the important things, we could be a lot further ahead.

Exercising this level of control will only strengthen one's character and ability to handle negative circumstances, rather than behaving like a loose cannon where no one knows where or when it will fire. The truth is, the erratic and uncontrolled behavior associated with the negative triggers will eventually backfire. So we need to stop, think and choose our response before we lose control.

Prayer

Our Most Gracious and Patient Heavenly Father, we do thank You for Your unconditional love towards us. Thank You for setting the example of how to respond to challenging and difficult situations. We trust that Your Words will be in our mouths (Jeremiah 1:9) so that we don't speak contrary to Your Word. Thank You for satisfying our mouths with all good things (Psalms 103:5), causing us to speak only that which is pleasing to You. We will not be like a brood of vipers being evil in our actions while speaking good things, because we know that out of the abundance of the heart, the mouth speaks (Matthew 12:34). Your Word says that vengeance is Yours and that You will repay (Romans 12:19), therefore, we will keep our tongues from speaking evil and we will seek and pursue peace (1 Peter 3:10-11). In Jesus' Name, Amen.

For He who would love life and see good days, let him refrain his tongue from evil, and his lips from speaking deceit. Let him turn away from evil and do good; let him seek peace and pursue it. 1 Peter 3:10-11

What are some areas of peace that you need to keep in your life?

_____

_____

_____

_____

_____

_____

_____

_____

_____

_____

_____

_____

_____

_____

_____

_____

_____

DAY EIGHT

More Than Enough

The human body fascinates me: its ability to push physical boundaries, its power to heal itself, its capacity to obtain and store information, and its agility and flexibility are just some of its phenomenal features. I'm reminded of when I had my first child and went through the different parenting courses. There was one on breastfeeding that left me speechless. As they discussed how the mother's body produces milk that provides everything the child would need on demand, I thought, my God has come up with everything. They would stress the importance of nursing in the early stages because the nutrients could not be mimicked in any formulas. They encouraged breastfeeding for as long as mother and baby could tolerate. In a recent read, I became further intrigued at the notion that breastfeeding was a supply and demand exchange. The more you feed, the more the baby is demanding from you and therefore, the more supply that's produced. Not only that, but also the bond and trust that is created between mother and child cannot be matched. The child anticipates that every time he/she requests food, the mother will produce and the child can eat until satisfied.

I love how one of the names and characters of God is El-Shaddai, God Almighty, Many-Breasted One; the God who supplies and whose supply never runs out. In essence, just like a mother supplies all that a child needs through the nursing process, so God, El-Shaddai, supplies all that we need; having enough supply for all His children and a supply that will never run dry.

Prayer

El-Shaddai, God Almighty (Genesis 17:1), the Many Breasted One; we come before You with thanksgiving and reverence. We love how You show us, through the natural exchanges of our human bodies and particularly that of a nursing mother, that You take care of us. We appreciate how You have thought of everything and have answered all questions even before they are asked. We thank You for abundantly supplying us with everything we need. We thank You that there is enough supply for all who demand it and that Your supply never runs dry (Isaiah 66:11). We rest upon Your Word and receive all the nourishment, nutrients and substance we need. We lay at Your feet to receive everything that You have for us. We do not move until we are satisfied (Psalms 36:8) and we continue to draw from Your supply. We don't take for granted what You have prepared for us and we look forward to an enjoyable feasting. In Jesus' Name, Amen.

> *When Abram was ninety-nine years old, the Lord appeared*
> *to Abram and said to him, "I am Almighty God; walk before*
> *Me and be blameless." Genesis 17:1*

Knowing that God Almighty has an unending supply, what can you ask Him to satisfy you with?

_____

_____

_____

_____

_____

_____

_____

_____

DAY NINE

Stand Out

What makes you different, unique or stand out? Would someone be able to look in a crowd and notice you? Does it matter to you if you blend in? For us to have been uniquely, fearfully and wonderfully made, it's amazing how many of us look the same, talk the same and are safely packaged in our comfort of similarity. Why are we so afraid to be who God created us to be, in our uniqueness and differences? We desire to be like other people and we covet what it appears others have, wishing we were dealt a different set of cards. It seems like it would be easier and less time consuming if we could just be who we were designed to be. What's wrong with who you are? What don't you like? What do you wish you could change? When God made us, He did it without apology and He certainly didn't make a mistake; but when we question who we were called and destined to be, it's like a slap in the face to God. Instead of trying to change what was purposed, let's accept and applaud our Creator's handiwork. Be you; you'll be the best you that ever was.

Prayer

Heavenly Father, You Who are perfect, we position ourselves and offer You the highest praise. You positioned the moon and stars, You were intentional on how the earth rotates around the sun. You are our destiny fulfiller and You make everything good. We are fearfully and wonderfully made; Your works are marvelous (Psalms 139:14). Who are we that You are mindful of us, and that You visit us (Psalms 8:4)? We will not second-guess who You are in and through us. The only thing we will covet is that the best gifts of the Spirit be operational in our lives. Help us to see the bigger picture and our place in it. We are Your vessels, molded and shaped (Jeremiah 18:4) into the masterpieces that we are, to be used for Your glory. Have Your way in us, oh God. In Jesus' Name, Amen.

> *And the vessel that he made of clay was marred in the hand*
> *of the potter; so he made it again into another vessel, as it*
> *seemed good to the potter to make. Jeremiah 18:4*

What do you like about yourself? What don't you like about yourself? Knowing that God made you without apology, does that change what you dislike about yourself?

_____

_____

_____

_____

_____

_____

_____

_____

_____

_____

_____

_____

_____

_____

_____

_____

_____

_____

_____

_____

DAY TEN

Find Your Peace

Have you ever been in a crowded area or space like an airport or mall? Did you feel uneasy, uncomfortable or unsettled? Have you ever had to just take a moment to collect your thoughts and get yourself together? Often, I have had to quiet my mind and gather myself in situations like that, because there's no other way to quiet the noise around me.

It's amazing the power we possess within ourselves; the power to focus, the power to control ourselves in uncontrollable situations and environments; the power to find our way amidst the inundation of thoughts and circumstances. The beauty of this power is that we are the ones in control of it! What do you do or where do you go to find your peace? We all have to locate what will bring us calm in a storm so that we don't succumb to the waves. Finding your peace could be anything from prayer, to reading, playing music, to exercising. Whatever it is, make sure it's solid, because the reality is, your reality is in your control.

Prayer

Heavenly Father, You are the Peace Giver. You are the Glory and Lifter of our heads. We find comfort in knowing that Christ's peace was left for our advantage and that it is superior to the peace of the world (John 14:27). We learn to quiet ourselves so that we can experience the peace within, allowing it to permeate. We do not allow out-of-control thinking to consume and distract us, for we have the mind of Christ (1 Corinthians 2:16). We allow Your peace to guard our hearts and minds, because we refuse to be anxious or worried (Philippians 4:6-7). In the midst of chaos, may the peace we possess keep us. In Jesus' Name, Amen.

31

> **Be anxious for nothing, but in everything by prayer and supplication, with thanksgiving, let your requests be made known to God; and the peace of God, which surpasses all understanding, will guard your hearts and minds through Christ Jesus. Philippians 4:6-7**

How do you find your peace amidst the chaos?

_____

_____

_____

_____

_____

_____

_____

_____

_____

_____

_____

_____

_____

_____

_____

_____

_____

_____

_____

DAY ELEVEN

Time Difference

I began traveling at a young age and one constant with travel is that there are differences in times/time zones. I was born and raised in Los Angeles, California, USA, which is on the west coast of the country. The west coast has a specific time zone that compliments the standard and daylight savings times for that region of the country, whereas a place like New York City, New York, which is still in the USA, is on the east coast of the country and has a completely different time zone. One could look at the east coast as three hours ahead of the west coast, or one could say the west coast is three hours behind the east coast.

If we parallel this to our lives; where we find ourselves compared to where other people are, it can appear that some are ahead of us in life and some are behind us. The truth is that we are all where we are because of the choices we made or choices that were made that effect us. Our day is our day, our time is our time and our moments are our moments. So instead of worrying about where others are and what others are doing, we should relish our moment and take advantage of the time we have been given.

Prayer

Our most Gracious Heavenly Father, we do thank You that our eternal destinies are linked to Your plans for our lives (Jeremiah 29:11). We keep consciously aware that You, being the Author of life (Acts 3:15 NIV) therefore the author of time, are keen on what is right for us, when it is right for us. We do not try and take matters into our own hands, and we do not covet the fruit of our neighbor's harvest (Exodus 20:17). We remain faithful to the call and assignment on our lives and we do not try to hurry up our process. There is a time for everything under heaven and earth; therefore, we are careful to maximize our moments, live in our now and stay in our lanes. Where we are is where we are supposed to be at this moment in time as we are being led by Your Spirit. In Jesus' Name, Amen.

> *For I know the thoughts that I think toward you, says the*
> *Lord, thoughts of peace and not of evil, to give you a future*
> *and a hope. Jeremiah 29:11*

If you were to tell your younger self anything about time, what would it be?

_____

_____

_____

_____

_____

_____

_____

_____

_____

_____

_____

_____

_____

_____

_____

_____

_____

_____

_____

_____

DAY TWELVE

Just A Moment

Have you ever just needed a moment; a break away from life's demands? It might be going on a walk, stopping and taking some deep breaths, talking it out, going on a vacation or having a good cry. I consider these "time outs" necessary for regrouping. Sometimes we go, go, go and it's as if we are running on fumes, and yet, we keep going. This behavior is unhealthy and can result in mental, emotional and physical burnout. What's important to remember is that we are human and our bodies and minds need refueling. Like a car, it can only go as far as the fuel that's in it; once the gas runs out, the car stops. The car isn't broken; it just needs a moment to be filled up again. In the same way, we are not broken; we just need a moment to refresh and refuel.

Prayer

Heavenly Father, we thank You for giving us the breath of life (Genesis 2:7). We breathe in the freshness of each new day, laced with new mercies (Lamentations 3:22-23). We take a time out to refresh and refuel so that we can fulfill the assignments that await us. We avoid burnout by identifying the triggers that can set us back. We keep ourselves charged spiritually, knowing that it will have a positive impact on us mentally, physically and emotionally. We find our rest in You (Matthew 11:29). We do not try to fix or fill ourselves, but we rely on Your wisdom to help us. Help us identify areas in which we need to refuel and show us how to mange our lives better. We find our complete rest and hope in You and we thank You for always being there for us. In Jesus' Name, Amen.

**Take My yoke upon you and learn from Me, for I am gentle
and lowly in heart, and you will find rest for your souls.
Matthew 11:29**

Take a moment and breathe knowing that you find your rest in God. Write down how that felt.

_____

_____

_____

_____

_____

_____

_____

_____

_____

_____

_____

_____

_____

_____

_____

_____

_____

_____

DAY THIRTEEN

Worship

Worship shifts the atmosphere, because as worshippers we set the atmosphere, the altar on which the presence of God can dwell. Worship is our posture of reverence towards our Heavenly Father, expressing our gratitude and trust in His Mighty power. We should worship when things are well and when things seem unwell; for we worship Him because of Who He is, not because of how we feel. In worshipping God because of Who He is, we know by His character and integrity that the things which aren't going well naturally will be made right by Him.

Worship is an escape, a game changer, and a manifested expression of who God is to us. We should take time throughout our day, not just the prescribed time we've set aside, to worship; worship on the drive to work, worship during a coffee break, worship while preparing dinner, washing the dishes, before going to bed; whenever you think about the wonder of Who God is, take a moment and offer worship. In doing this, our attitude and posture has to change, because it's no longer focused on us, but Him.

Prayer

Heavenly Father, You are the Most High God. You have set Your Name above all names (Philippians 2:9) and we worship You. Who You are is worthy of all glory, honor and praise. We shift things with our worship. We set the atmosphere with our worship, preparing an altar where You can dwell. Our worship gets Your attention and gives You access into our lives and situations, for true worshippers worship You in spirit and in truth (John 4:24). Our worship shifts our feelings from self and completely onto You. We release worship as a confirmation that we trust You to work all things together for our good, for we love You and are called according to Your purpose (Romans 8:28). We find our victory in You, therefore, our worship is perpetual. May You receive our worship today. In Jesus' Name, Amen.

> *God is Spirit, and those who worship Him must worship in*
> *spirit and truth. John 4:24*

As a true worshipper, take some time and worship God because of Who He is. Write down Who He is to you.

_____

_____

_____

_____

_____

_____

_____

_____

_____

_____

_____

_____

_____

_____

_____

_____

_____

_____

_____

DAY FOURTEEN

Pacify

All three of our children were given a pacifier/dummy when they were smaller in order to calm and comfort them if they became agitated. Not everyone believes in the idea of these brilliant tools, but for me, they have worked wonders. It's as if our children knew that these "gifts from God" would make all things better. They would use them when they cried, when they were uncomfortable or when they would want to go to sleep. It would bring them such a peace. Much like these little jewels, we need to allow the Word of God to pacify us; help us to calm our agitations, anxieties, fears and ultimately bring us to a place of peace. It always amazed me how our children would literally fight to get these pacifiers in their mouths just so that they could find their comfort. In the same way, we should fight to get God's Word in our mouths and find rest.

Prayer

Heavenly Father, our Giver of rest (Exodus 33:14), we remain safe and comforted under Your mighty hand. Your sovereignty brings about a serenity that we cannot comprehend. We eat and drink Your Word, allowing Your Word to become all the spiritual nourishment we could ever need. We need Your presence with us, everywhere we go, or we do not go up from here (Exodus 33:15). Help us experience You in new and fresh ways, and may we thrive because we are made in Your likeness and image (Genesis 1:26). You satisfy and nurture us as we hunger and thirst for You, and You truly make all things better. In Jesus' Name, Amen.

And He said, "My Presence will go with you, and I will give you rest." Exodus 33:14

What scripture can you meditate on today to pacify your agitations, anxieties, uncertainties and fears?

_____

_____

_____

_____

_____

_____

_____

_____

_____

_____

_____

_____

_____

_____

_____

_____

_____

_____

_____

_____

_____

_____

_____

_____

_____

_____

DAY FIFTEEN

Money Isn't Everything

I used to think that money would solve everything, make me happy and get me whatever I wanted, as many people do. However, having money and not having money, I've realized that money doesn't have as much power as we think. It may buy the material things, but it definitely doesn't buy happiness, peace, soundness of mind, genuine relationships and long life. There's nothing wrong with money, I would actually like more of it; but I understand that money shouldn't change who I am and doesn't change my purpose.

For me, money resources purpose. There are far too many people with lots of money that don't live fulfilled lives and many people without a lot of money, whose lives couldn't be better. So what's the deal? I believe money complicates the lives of those who are looking for their fulfillment in it. When someone is fulfilled, with or without money, then money can't rule them. Aside from all of that, we can't take any money or anything money can buy with us when we die. So I'd rather live in my fulfilled purpose and let money be an accessory to my fulfillment.

Prayer

Heavenly Father, we thank You for Your goodness, Your mercy and Your grace. There is no one like You, God. We acknowledge You as the reason why we live, move and have our being (Acts 17:28). We allow Your Spirit within us to lead and guide us into all truth (John 16:13). We don't let external factors establish our security in this life, but we find our complete security in You. We remember You, Lord our God, for You have given us the power to obtain wealth, that Your covenant may be established (Deuteronomy 8:18). We therefore put our complete faith and trust in You and not in material things. We use what You give us to fulfill purpose and not self-greed and gratification. We do not look at the things that are seen, for they are temporary; but we look at the things that are unseen, for they are eternal (2 Corinthians 4:18). Help us find our purpose in You and not in the things of this world. In Jesus' Name, Amen.

> *While we do not look at the things which are seen, but at the things which are not seen. For the things which are seen are temporary, but the things which are not seen are eternal.*
> *2 Corinthians 4:18*

What are some things in your life that give you purpose, which money can't buy?

_____

_____

_____

_____

_____

_____

_____

_____

_____

_____

_____

_____

_____

_____

_____

_____

_____

_____

Power in Prayer

What are you praying for right now? What are you believing God for and who are the people standing with you? Sometimes, people ask us to pray for them and we forget, and there are times we ask others to pray for us and we aren't sure whether they will or not. We must commit to praying for and being in agreement with one another, that God will answer our prayers, for we know that when two agree on earth concerning anything, it will be done by the Father. Prayer is one of the most powerful tools we have in our arsenals as believers, and it is even greater when we can stand in agreement with one another. God is faithful and whatever it is we desire, we must ask Him in faith, believing that He not only exists but that He also cares enough to respond to those who diligently seek Him.

Prayer

Heavenly Father, we thank You for Your awesome splendor and a love that can't be explained. We thank You that we are Your chosen people and that Your ears are open to our prayers (2 Chronicles 7:15). We don't always know what to pray for as we ought, but we have Jesus, Who is always interceding on our behalf (Romans 8:26) and that is more than we could ever ask for. We thank You for the power we have in prayer and that our prayers, according to Your Word, move You to respond. Just as Christ intercedes for us, so we pray for one another. Father, we pray for whoever is reading this, that You would bless them and keep them; that whatever they are believing You for, in line with Your Word, it shall be done. We come against any interference that would hinder our prayers from being answered. We thank You for hearing us and Your willingness to respond (Hebrews 11:6 MSG). In Jesus' Name, Amen.

> **Likewise the Spirit also helps in our weaknesses. For we do
> not know what we should pray for as we ought, but the
> Spirit Himself makes intercession for us with groanings which
> cannot be uttered. Romans 8:26**

God answers prayers. What can you ask God for today and who can you
have stand in agreement with you for your prayers to be answered?

_____

_____

_____

_____

_____

_____

_____

_____

_____

_____

_____

_____

_____

_____

_____

_____

_____

_____

_____

DAY SEVENTEEN

Don't Be Scared

I don't recall when my children began to express fear of sleeping in their rooms alone, being afraid of the dark or being scared to walk from one room to another by themselves. What I do recall are my efforts to encourage bravery, even though I myself have yet to master complete fearlessness. At some point we have all been scared of something or someone and no matter how often I tell my children that there is nothing to be afraid of, they still have moments when they're struck by fear. What I find interesting is the bravery, courage and boldness that comes over them when they're accompanied by someone. Nothing has changed in instruction, destination or assignment, but knowing someone is with them tends to eliminate or at least minimize the fear.

Isn't this true for us, when God says that He will never leave us nor forsake us? Why then do we allow fear to hinder our faith? We are constantly encouraged by God's Word in the area of eliminating fear and embracing faith as a way of life. Be encouraged that as you step away from fear, you can be immersed in faith and it's faith that will springboard you into your purpose and destiny.

Prayer

Heavenly Father, we rejoice in You always, for You turn our mourning into dancing and our sorrow into joy. You give us beauty for ashes (Isaiah 61:3) and a song of praise in the midst of adversity. We let not our hearts be troubled, neither do we let them be afraid, for Your peace is with us (John 14:27). We no longer allow fear a place in our lives, for it is our faith that pleases You (Hebrews 11:6) and that is all we desire. We will not be afraid nor dismayed, for You are with us wherever we go (Joshua 1:9). We speak peace and eliminate fear from having any place. We thank You for never leaving us or forsaking us (Deuteronomy 31:6). In Jesus' Name, Amen.

Have I not commanded you? Be strong and of good courage;
do not be afraid, nor be dismayed, for the Lord your God is
with you wherever you go. Joshua 1:9

What fears do you need to eliminate from your life?

_____

_____

_____

_____

_____

_____

_____

_____

_____

_____

_____

_____

_____

_____

_____

_____

_____

_____

_____

_____

_____

DAY EIGHTEEN

Grow Up

One speaks with their actions long before one speaks with their words. Think about it — a baby cannot articulate in words what he/she wants, but through actions and cries, the parent can try and decipher what may be wrong. Parents tend to try different things like feeding, changing, giving attention, rocking, or whatever they think will work in order to calm or satisfy the baby.

In the body of Christ, we often take on these baby-like characteristics, acting out or not articulating what's going on with hopes that someone, anyone, even God, will guess what's wrong. We force people to participate in our game of charades and then get upset when they don't play along, so much so that we use their inability to figure out what's wrong with us as justification to our childish tantrums. I wonder if we would have greater outcomes if we would express our feelings, share our offenses and maturely and decisively "get over it." The Word speaks of when we were children, we spoke and acted as such; but with maturity, we put away childish things. It's "time out" for adults acting like children. Stop blaming your shortcomings on others' inabilities to encrypt your secret codes. You started the game, never asking if one wanted to play. It's time to put away the childish things and mature into the total being God created you to be.

Prayer

Heavenly Father, You are our solid Rock! We can lean on You, trust in You and You will not move. We do not rely on our own ability, as our ability will limit us in reaching our destinies. Lord, we ask that You help us grow up in the things of You. We will not allow immaturity and childish behavior to cripple us or be our crutch, delaying progress. For we no longer act or speak as children, and we put away childish things (1 Corinthians 13:11). You have given us words and specifically Your Word to use as our way to communicate with You and others. We have been given a voice; therefore we don't allow the enemy to snatch it away. We allow our words and our actions to compliment each other (James 1:22). We don't allow our actions to speak for us, and we don't allow our words to be proxy for our actions. What we say, we do, and what we do, we say. With Your help, we know that all things are possible (Luke 18:27). We thank You for it now. In Jesus' Name, Amen.

> *When I was a child, I spoke as a child, I understood as a child,*
> *I thought as a child; but when I became a man, I put away*
> *childish things. 1 Corinthians 13:11*

What childish behaviors do you need to do away with?

_____

_____

_____

DAY NINETEEN

If the Shoe Fits

I'm sure we've all heard the statement "if the shoe fits, wear it." This statement promotes the idea that if something belongs or pertains to you, whether good or bad, then accept it. When one accepts responsibility for an action which has consequences, this can be seen as a negative, whereas a Cinderella story, where a literal shoe fitting is considered a dream come true.

Oftentimes, we try and fit into something that doesn't fit us; we internalize and harbor missteps, misfortunes and downfalls but those don't have to fit into our way of living. The danger in force fitting is that it can cause more damage and pain than necessary. If it fits, it fits, you don't have to force it; but if it doesn't, then let it be. God never intended for us to fit into the mold of this world, but rather be transformed by His Word. Be careful not to become victim to the systems set by this world, but be free, because whom the Son sets free, is free indeed.

Prayer

Heavenly Father, we acknowledge You as Perfect and All-knowing. You set the earth in orbit and made everything fit in its place. There are no accidents in You. We thank You that our most precious gift is that of Jesus (John 3:16) and in Him, all things are made new. We will not conform to fit in with the ways of this world because we are transformed by the renewing of our minds (Romans 12:2), and that being Your Word. We know that with every action there is a reaction and we must choose wisely. We format ourselves to the conditions of Your Word without apology or complaint. You are the Potter and we are the clay, the work of Your hand (Isaiah 64:8) and we therefore refuse to allow ourselves to be shaped, molded or made to fit into anything that is contrary to your original intent. We thank You that Your perfect work is done in us. In Jesus' Name, Amen.

> *And do not be conformed to this world, but be transformed*
> *by the renewing of your mind, that you may prove what is*
> *that good and acceptable and perfect will of God.*
> *Romans 12:2*

What have you tried to make fit in your life?

_____

_____

_____

_____

_____

_____

_____

_____

_____

_____

_____

_____

_____

_____

_____

_____

_____

_____

_____

DAY TWENTY

Shift

Driving a manual car is very different and a lot more involved than driving an automatic. One thing that I have noticed when driving a manual, is that in order to accelerate, you have to shift gears. You can't be in first gear and expect to reach high speeds without consequence. It is imperative that one moves the gears to the necessary positions in order to maximize the ease of driving. When I first learned how to drive manually, I found out quickly that I couldn't make the car do anything more than it was structured to do, no matter how badly I wanted it.

In parallel, we must learn how to adjust and shift our thinking if we want to move ahead quickly. We can't do more than we are able and the only way we know what we are capable of is when we get moving. Just like a manual car won't go beyond its point of ability, neither will we. This is why we need the help of the Holy Spirit, to add His super ability to our natural ability, allowing us to accelerate beyond what we can do on our own. Be willing to shift in order to propel.

Prayer

Dear Heavenly Father, greater are You in us than he that is in the world (1 John 4:4). We thank You for allowing us to be who You created us to be and we walk in that freedom. We know that we have limitations when it comes to our natural abilities, therefore we seek you to do exceedingly, abundantly above all that we could ever ask or think, according to Your Power that works in us (Ephesians 3:20). We shift our thinking and align our thoughts to Yours, in order that we may move ahead at the appropriate speed bypassing delays and setbacks. We rely on Your Spirit to direct and set us on the right course for our lives. We don't limit ourselves because we have the Mind of Christ (Philippians 2:5), which gives us the wisdom to live this life victoriously. In Jesus' Name, Amen.

> *Let this mind be in you which was also in Christ Jesus.*
> **Philippians 2:5**

In what areas can you shift your thinking, so that your thoughts align with God's thoughts for you?

_____

_____

_____

_____

_____

_____

_____

_____

_____

_____

_____

_____

_____

_____

_____

_____

_____

_____

_____

_____

DAY TWENTY-ONE

Because I'm Happy

I was the parent that felt like, if one of my kids received something, so should the other. For instance, if we were at the store and my son got a sweet, so would my daughter. For Christmas, if my daughter got two outfits and a toy, then my son would get two outfits and a toy. It even got to the point when it was one of their birthdays and I would try to make sure there was a gift for the other one as well. This soon created an expectation that one should always have what the other has. My husband showed me how this method of thinking and display of giving was not healthy nor realistic. It took me a while to accept this truth, but the reality is, we don't all get what others have and we must be careful not to expect that it should be this way.

The biggest lesson for me to have learned and to teach our children was the action of being happy for someone when they received something even if we didn't. Oftentimes, we can be happy for someone when we have something as well, but what if we didn't have something; does that mean we can't celebrate someone who does? We would certainly want someone to be happy for us when we receive something.

The Bible tells us to rejoice with those who rejoice. This wasn't always easy for our kids to accept and understand, and from time to time, we must remind them that just because one has something doesn't automatically guarantee that the other will have it also or that it will be equal. We will all have our time of receiving; the question becomes whether we can be happy for someone else who has received while we are waiting for our turn?

Prayer

Heavenly Father, what a Mighty God You are. We are privileged to serve You and be called Your children. Heaven and earth rejoice (1 Chronicles 16:31) and respond to Your commands and we make it a point to do the same. Thank You for establishing principles that allow us to grow and develop into the mature people You have destined us to be. We know that every good and perfect gift comes from You (James 1:17) and that we will all receive what is due. Therefore, we do not become sour or bitter when others are blessed. Rather, we rejoice and are glad because we know that as we rejoice with those who rejoice (Romans 12:15), we will reap what we have sown when it is our time. We do not covet what others have because it is tailored for them. We focus on what is for us and do not allow the enemy to drive a wedge between we, Your children, over gifts that You, our Father, have given. Thank You for freely giving to all of us the gift of Jesus (Ephesians 4:7), a Gift that we can all rejoice in receiving. In Jesus' Name, Amen.

> *Every good gift and every perfect gift is from above, and comes down from the Father of lights, with whom there is no variation or shadow of turning. James 1:17*

Who can you rejoice with and be happy for that has received an answer to their prayer?

_____

_____

_____

_____

_____

_____

_____

DAY TWENTY-TWO

Switch

I've learned a very important lesson in life which pertains to dwelling on a thought that has the potential to bring me down instead of lift me up. This lesson wasn't something I practiced, but rather found myself teaching other people. The lesson is simply switching your negative thoughts to positive ones. Whenever my children would hurt themselves or be upset about something, I found myself quickly encouraging them to think of something that was the complete opposite. In counseling appointments, I would have a person count to ten out loud and then interrupt them by asking a question. This method would cause them to forget about counting and focus on answering the question. The principle is simple: we have the power to change or switch our thoughts immediately by thinking or doing something opposite to the thought that is trying to weigh us down.

I was battling with some quite severe negative thoughts; I was even to the point of tears. In that moment I realized the more I sat there thinking about it, the sadder I became. I asked God to help me get over those feelings. In fact, this method that I'm constantly encouraging others to do was what I needed to do in that moment and that I did. I jumped up, changed my thinking and went into a place where my thoughts were consumed by something enjoyable. This action put the negative thoughts to rest, and revived positive and healthy thoughts. I felt so much better and realized the power we posses with our thoughts. Try it: if a negative thought attempts to violate your mind space, change your position by thinking or doing something positive.

Prayer

Lord, help us to free ourselves from the bondage of negative thoughts. We don't just pray the thoughts away, but we are sure to replace the negative consuming thoughts with that of Your Word, for we know that is where our transformation takes place (Romans 12:2). We dwell on things that are true, noble, just, pure, lovely, of good report, virtuous, and praiseworthy (Philippians 4:8), so that there is no room for anything contrary. We thank You for the power we have with our words (Proverbs 18:21) and we choose life by thinking and speaking life-giving thoughts and words. May we speak based on what we practice and not just practice what we say. In Jesus' Name, Amen.

> *Finally, brethren, whatever things are true, whatever things are noble, whatever things are just, whatever things are pure, whatever things are lovely, whatever things are of good report, if there is any virtue and if there is anything praiseworthy — meditate on these things. Philippians 4:8*

When negative thoughts come, read this scripture aloud and write down the positive, true, noble, just, pure, lovely, virtuous and praiseworthy thoughts to counteract the negative ones.

_____

_____

_____

_____

_____

_____

_____

_____

_____

_____

Loyalty

Friendships are made up of many different qualities, and I believe one characteristic that is universal in true friendship, is loyalty. Loyalty, by definition, is the quality of showing firm and constant support or allegiance to a person or institution; however, I find this definition is often blurred. I have found that people have made loyalty a temporary, faded and loose term. Posting a picture of someone with kind words isn't loyalty; disliking someone because a friend dislikes them isn't loyalty; and showing up when convenient isn't loyalty. It's very difficult for me to believe someone who proclaims loyalty with their words but not their actions, having come to accept that people speak with their actions long before they speak with their words.

When it's all said and done, does the idea of loyalty count if our loyalty to others means our disloyalty to God? Our first priority is being loyal to God by following Him and doing what He says. In perfecting this loyalty, we are taught how to be loyal to one another. Our structure of thinking can't be solely based on our interactions with our fellow man to the exclusion of our Creator. Our character traits shouldn't be measured by man's standards or definitions, but rather based on the nature, character and definitions that God Himself outlined. By Biblical definition, loyalty is the commitment to an ongoing relationship and to the attitude and behavior demanded by it. This being the case, our loyalty should be a complete commitment to perfection, wholeness, safety and peace. So, the next time this word is used or heard, we should funnel it through the filter of how God intended it.

Prayer

Oh God, help us to set our filter to Who You are and what You desire over that of man. We are made in the very likeness and image of You (Genesis 1:26) therefore, we want to see things based on how You see them. Forgive us for redefining things to suit our comforts and help us to make a point of checking our lives against Your Word. We are not just hearers of Your Word, but we are doers (James 1:22). We allow Your Word to define the patterns of our lives and behaviors. Our hearts are loyal to You; we walk in Your statues and we keep Your commandments (2 Chronicles 25:2) in order that our commitment, attitude and behavior aim towards the complete wholeness, perfection, safety and peace that You so desire. In Jesus' Name, Amen.

> **But be doers of the word, and not hearers only, deceiving yourselves. James 1:22**

How do you define loyalty? Does it compliment God's definition of loyalty?

_____

_____

_____

_____

_____

_____

_____

_____

_____

_____

_____

_____

_____

DAY TWENTY-FOUR

Write It Down

There is something really important about writing things down. Whether it is a reminder about an appointment, an idea or grocery list; research proves that writing things down helps one retain the information better and for a longer period of time. I remember there being a time before technology became what it is today, that our way of communication was through writing notes instead of text messages or e-mails. With technological advancements, one can still capture their thoughts, but for me, there is nothing like putting pen to paper. Whatever your particular preference, take a moment and write something down: write down a dream, desire, prayer, positive affirmation or note to someone. Write down something that you can go back to as a reference, a reminder or an encouragement. You might be surprised at how writing it down gives you a connection between what's inside of you and what you want to see manifest for you or someone else. The Bible speaks about writing things down and making it plain so that those who read it can run with it. This encourages me that what I write down has the potential to come to pass, not only with what I do to make it happen, but with what others may be able to do who read it. Give it a shot – jot something down today.

Prayer

Almighty God, we worship You today. We thank You for Your manifested presence in our lives and situations. Thank You for overwhelming us with all good things and withholding nothing from us (Psalms 84:11). Our hearts are filled with praise. We take heed of Your Word and are sure to be doers of it and not just hearers (James 1:22), applying the truth of Your Word with action. We write down the vision You have given us and we make it plain so they that read it may run with it helping to bring it to pass (Habakkuk 2:2). We acknowledge Your Word as the ultimate truth and remain students of Your Word. We liken our tongue to that of the pen of a ready writer, ready and willing to write on the tablets of the hearts of Your people. We take our cue from You as the Author and Finisher of our faith and we thank You for making our story complete. In Jesus' Name, Amen.

> *Then the Lord answered me and said: "Write the vision And make it plain on tablets, That he may run who reads it."*
> *Habakkuk 2:2*

Write down a dream, vision, prayer, positive affirmation or encouragement. Come back and read it in a week and see the impact it makes.

_____

_____

_____

_____

_____

_____

_____

_____

_____

_____

_____

_____

_____

_____

_____

_____

_____

_____

DAY TWENTY-FIVE

The Underdog

I have this thing for the underdog. You know, the one who is outcast, looked over, not able to really fend for themselves, the ones in the background, kind of quiet and unassuming. I'm not completely sure why I tend to be drawn to them, but it's been this way for a while. What I've come to notice is that as I'm trying to "save" the one who appears unable to save themselves, I neglect the "over dog," the one I think can fend for themselves, is strong willed, vocal and upfront. I learned a valuable lesson; people are people and all people need the same extension of love and attention. Sometimes, the over compensation for the underdog can cause the neglect and demise of the one who is not the underdog.

People can sense when you are unsupportive, not interested, negligent or different towards them; and because we were not created to be mind readers, we don't always know or understand why. Simply put, there is nothing wrong with being a voice to the voiceless, friend to the friendless, and hope for the hopeless; but we should remember and consider that everyone needs love and affection and should not be neglected just because they seem like they have it all together. There's a quote I read online (author unknown) that says, "The worst part about being strong is that no one ever asks if you're okay." Let's be people who are sensitive to everyone, no matter where they may seem to rank on the "I'm okay" scale.

Prayer

Heavenly Father, the One who knows our inward and outward beings better than we know them ourselves; we thank You for creating us unique and special. Thank You for not treating us based on our level of social status, but for loving us all the same, for You show no bias or partiality. Help us to see others the way You see them and help us to be what they need in that moment (Romans 15:1 NIV). We thank You for Your Strength being made perfect in our weakness because of Your all-sufficient grace (2 Corinthians 12:9). Help us to extend grace and not neglect others because we think they have it all together. We ask that Your Spirit would lead us and give us discernment to be all things to all people so that we may win some. We pray for those who may not have the voice to speak up for themselves or the courage to defend, and we also pray for those who have the voice to defend themselves, but find themselves not being okay. Strengthen us by Your Word and may we be encouraged daily that You are for us (Romans 8:31). In Jesus' Name, Amen.

> *May the God who gives endurance and encouragement give you the same attitude of mind toward each other that Christ Jesus had. Romans 15:5*

Write down the names of people in your world who seem to have it together and also those who seem to not have it together. Make a point of checking on them this week.

_____

_____

_____

_____

_____

_____

_____

_____

_____

_____

_____

_____

DAY TWENTY-SIX

Cut It Off

I used to be a hairdresser and I love the beauty and creativity that comes from a new hairstyle. Though I don't practice hairstyling as a profession anymore, I still very much enjoy creating new looks on my daughters and myself. Just the other day, I was playing around with my hair and realized how much it had grown. What I also noticed was that there was a lot of damage to the ends of my hair. Even though it was long, it wasn't healthy and was in need of a serious trim. Without a second thought, I grabbed a pair of scissors and cut off all the dead ends.

I remember a time where I would have preferred to keep the ugly, scraggly ends, just for the sake of length but that was so foolish. In keeping those dead ends, it negatively affected the good parts of my hair. It was like the dead ends would creep up and start to damage the good hair; so in my attempt to hold on to something, it was doing more harm than good. Now, when I see these ends that give the appearance of long hair, I cut them off, because it's simply an appearance and not the reality. Yes, my hair may not be as long once cut, but it certainly looks healthier and gives my hair a chance to grow back stronger than ever because it doesn't have anything compromising it.

We can easily equate this "hair" example to our lives. There are things we may be holding on to that appear healthy, when in actual fact, they're eating away at what's really good in our lives. It may be time for a trim.

Prayer

Heavenly Father, You are so good to us. You take care of every aspect of our lives, even the things we can't comprehend. We forget those things which are behind us and reach forward to those which are ahead (Philippians 3:13) because we know that our latter is greater than the past (Haggai 2:9). We are not holding onto things that do not produce fruit and we equally prune and cut back the things that bear fruit in order that it bear more (John 15:2). We know that You never intended the things You made to fail; we therefore stay activate in our pursuit to produce and allow You to prune us so that we may come to the full maturity in which You have ordained beforehand. In Jesus' Name, Amen.

Every branch in Me that does not bear fruit He takes away;
and every branch that bears fruit He prunes, that it may bear
more fruit. John 15:2

What things do you need to cut back or trim in order for them to grow and produce more?

_____

_____

_____

_____

_____

_____

_____

_____

_____

_____

_____

_____

_____

DAY TWENTY-SEVEN

Too Big

Have you ever dismissed a thought or an idea because it just seemed too big or out of your league? You thought it would be nice, but maybe for someone else who is more qualified, educated or well off than you? Why do we disqualify ourselves from being able to do the big and impossible things? Are we afraid of failing or of the work that may be required to put into it? Do you ever wonder why the thought has come to you in the first place?

I believe that ideas, thoughts, concepts and dreams come to us because we are capable to bring them to pass. However, we tend to sabotage and discount ourselves for one reason or another. If we understand that we are incapable of succeeding on our own and that we need the help of our Creator, maybe we would be more persistent in pursuing these thoughts in making them a reality. Dreams are to be dreamt and making dreams come true becomes the responsibility of the Dream Giver, because where we can't, He can and He will. So before we dismiss or excuse another idea because of our fear of being inadequate, we should consult with the One who can do the impossible.

Prayer

Dear God, we thank You for Your Infinite wisdom, power and might. Great are You Lord, whose sun lights the sky by day and whose moon cools the earth by night. How Majestic and Wondrous are Your Works, Oh God. What You have made stands to be showcased and awed. You are the Dream Giver and You do the impossible (Luke 1:37). Our faith in You allows us to please You and have confidence when we come to You, believing that You are a Rewarder of those who diligently seek You (Hebrews 11:6). We no longer attempt to disqualify or

65

talk ourselves out of being able to obtain, achieve and succeed in whatever we put our minds to, for we know that as a man thinks in his heart, so is he (Proverbs 23:7). We thank you for placing dreams in us and for helping to bring those dreams to past. In Jesus' Name, Amen.

For with God nothing will be impossible. Luke 1:37

Write down a dream that seems too big to obtain, then pray and ask God to make what seems impossible, possible.

_____

_____

_____

_____

_____

_____

_____

_____

_____

_____

_____

_____

_____

_____

_____

_____

_____

_____

_____

DAY TWENTY-EIGHT

Heal Our Land

When we look at the news and see the havoc that is plaguing the world, it can strike up fear, panic and uncertainty within us. People that have never seen or experienced such devastation now find themselves displaced and seeking shelter, as the rest of the world looks on with concern. It's like one event after another, where people are coming to the aid of others they may not know or may never meet. A spirit of unity and compassion swept the nation to help those who have lost everything. Prayers are being offered up around the clock and a hope that the damage done and the work needed to restore it will be met with the same fervency and urgency in the aftermath.

It's a beautiful thing to see, how even in the face of adversity, people of all races, nationalities, religions and demographics come together to help others. As much as disaster has brought people together, to help those in need, so I have seen and experienced first hand the generosity of people extending a hand, even without disaster. For me, the greatest thing is the ability we have as people to help one another; that all in all, we can put aside our differences to lend a hand. Disaster and devastation should not be the only times we express the genuine good we possess as people, but should be an expectation that comes as a result of this beautiful quality called loved. Let goodness be named among us as we show and extend love to all those we come in contact with.

Prayer

Heavenly Father, we seek You and Your Kingdom first, above all (Matthew 6:33). We acknowledge You as the Most High God, Whose generosity sets a standard that can't be matched. We pray for healing and restoration for the world, whether in a state, by disaster or circumstance. May all resources be available to rebuild better than it was before. We speak peace because it is Your peace that has been left for us to obtain (John 14:27). We speak and live Your Word and allow Your Word to be the healing and cure the world needs. We humble ourselves and pray, seeking Your face and turning from our ways of wickedness, so that You may hear from heaven, forgive our sins and heal our land (2 Chronicles 7:14). May Your Kingdom come and Your will be done on earth, as it is in heaven (Mark 4:39). In Jesus' Name, Amen.

> *If My people who are called by My Name will humble themselves, and pray and seek My face, and turn from their wicked ways, then I will hear from heaven, and will forgive their sin and heal their land. 2 Chronicles 7:14*

Whether by disaster or circumstance, what good can you do today to help someone in need?

_____

_____

_____

_____

_____

_____

_____

_____

_____

_____

_____

_____

_____

_____

DAY TWENTY-NINE

So Let It Be

There are some things that are out of our control, things that we won't be able to manipulate, change or make go away. There are some things that just have to happen. I have realized that the one thing I can control is how I handle the situations that are out of my control. A true testament of one's faith can be seen in situations where no skill, education, financial or political status can change what happens and yet one still trusts that God will provide whatever is needed. What may seem like a dead-end or hopeless situation is an opportunity for God to show His power and might. God will restore, God will avenge and God will do just what He said He would do. He is never failing, His timing is perfect and His thoughts towards us are good and not evil. He desires to show us His limitless, unconditional love but we have to be willing to accept it and say so let it be!

Whatever it is, trust and believe; with God you will always come out above only and never beneath.

Prayer

Heavenly Father, we know that no eye has seen, nor ear heard, nor has entered into the hearts of those that love you, that in which You have planned (1 Corinthians 2:9). We therefore, take this opportunity to thank You for giving us an opportunity to be called Your own. Thank You for thinking good of us, for giving us a future and a hope (Jeremiah 29:11). We are excitedly awaiting the bountiful blessings that will overtake us being Your chosen people. We are incapable of controlling everything, but what we can control, we do with Your help. We lift up our eyes to the hills for that is where our help comes from (Psalms

121:1). Thank You for remaining the same, yesterday, today and forevermore. In Jesus' Name, Amen.

> *But as it is written: "Eye has not seen, nor ear heard, nor have entered into the heart of man the things which God has prepared for those who love Him." 1 Corinthians 2:9*

What is a situation that is out of your control, which you choose to allow God to take care of?

_____

_____

_____

_____

_____

_____

_____

_____

_____

_____

_____

_____

_____

_____

_____

_____

_____

_____

_____

_____

DAY THIRTY

Airy

One of the greatest lessons I've learned is that you can determine the true substance of a person by how they speak. I'm not talking about the pitch and tone of their voice, I'm talking about the content and the passion; does what they say add up with how they live? We've heard the statement "talk is cheap" and it is if there's no substance backing it up. Being full of substance would mean that your words and actions form a beautiful marriage. If you're not sure how this looks, find out what God's Word says about you and begin to speak that because His Word is sure to fill us to full and overflowing!

Prayer

Heavenly Father, You spoke the Words that created the Universe, and You breathed the breath of life that gives us life (Genesis 2:7), therefore we are packaged with everything that we have need of. We carefully seal off all entrances to our hearts and minds with Your peace (Philippians 4:7), leaving no room for being filled with the wrong things. The only thing we desire is to be full of You and Your Spirit, for Your Spirit leads and guides us into all truth (John16:13). We will not fluff ourselves up with meaningless, insignificant, idle conversation or thinking in order to protect the gift that is in us. May the beauty of who You are in us, be all the fullness we'll ever need. In Jesus' Name, Amen.

And the peace of God, which passeth all understanding, shall keep your hearts and minds through Christ Jesus.
Philippians 4:7

What is taking up space in your life? What areas do you need to allow God to fill and seal?

_____

_____

_____

_____

_____

_____

_____

_____

_____

_____

_____

_____

_____

_____

_____

_____

_____

_____

_____

_____

_____

_____

_____

_____

_____

_____

_____

_____

DAY THIRTY-ONE

Faith Smoothies

I just love it how God speaks to me. It's truly like a conversation with my Father. He uses practical, everyday examples to make what He says relevant and relatable. He uses my children (yes, my children), when I'm cooking, doing a puzzle, walking, gymming, and so much more. One particular morning as I was preparing my breakfast, God began to correlate life to the process of making a smoothie. When making a smoothie, most items are frozen and mixed with a liquid. In order for everything to mix well, I have to be sure to break up the frozen elements to get the preferred texture, and this takes time and strategy. I usually begin by using a setting on the blender to break up the solids. I may have to do this a few times before adding any additional elements. Once I break the solids up enough, I transition the blender to another setting in order to get everything incorporated. When everything blends together nicely, I have the perfect smoothie.

The correlation is that faith is like a smoothie. You take all the ingredients: the Word of God, your situation (the hard, solid, frozen stuff), confidence, worship, confession and seed; mix it all together and eventually the hard stuff gets chopped up, broken down and turned into a smooth and satisfying victory! Praise God!

Prayer

Heavenly Father, we know that we as the just must live by faith (Hebrews 10:38) and our faith is activated by Your Word. We therefore take all of the things that are hard, difficult or discouraging, and place them before You. We allow Your Word to chop up and break down those things that were meant to discourage us and use them to develop and cultivate us into the true faith giants that You intended. We know that faith without works is dead (James 2:26), so we charge and exercise our faith by acting on what we believe, and what we believe is Your Word. Thank You for the practical examples that we encounter everyday that let us know that You are real and desire a real relationship with us. May we be stronger than ever because of Your Word (Psalms 119:28). In Jesus' Name, Amen.

> *For as the body without the spirit is dead, so faith without works is dead also. James 2:26*

What are some practical, everyday things that God can use to show you how to live by faith?

_____

_____

_____

_____

_____

_____

_____

_____

_____

_____

_____

_____

_____

_____

_____

_____

_____

www.ingramcontent.com/pod-product-compliance
Lightning Source LLC
Chambersburg PA
CBHW031526040426
42445CB00009B/410